2007

2006

The Journey Within

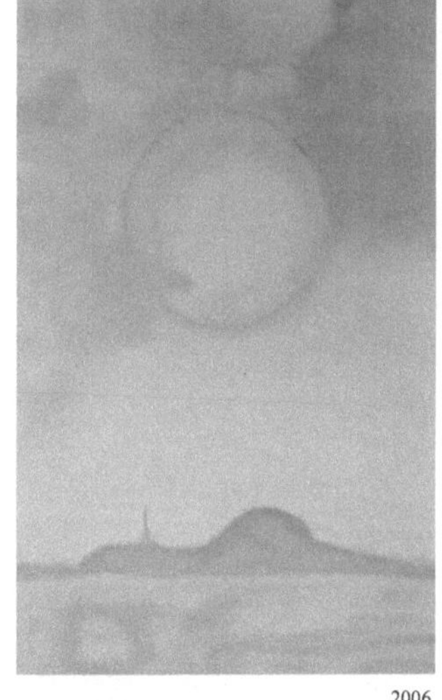

2006

2006

By Debora Rodante

The Journey Within
Written by Deborah Rodante, RN

First Printing
Printed in the United States of America

Published by Olmstead Publishing
1631 Rock Springs Road
Apopka, FL 32712-2229
olmsteadllc@usa.com

The UPS Store
1631 Rock Springs Road
Apopka, FL 32712-2229
store5514@theupsstore.com

ISBN 1-934194-20-4
978-1-934194-20-1

I dedicate this book to my loving, beautiful daughter, Rachel. Her heart radiates love into my life each day.

My heartfelt thanks to my husband, Douglas, for inspiring me and being my mentor.

SOLICE

I awaken from slumber with threads of my identity woven into new patterns. The colors resonate with those of tranquillity, the clothes I wear anointed with renewed spirit and energy. I ponder the distant dreams of masked happiness and solitude, the warrior and I have reunited at last. My eyes burn in defense of the fictional novels I once read.

I choose to stay between the lines of the path that has opened for me. I choose to trust only the meditations of my heart. I catapult over the black statues that used to block me and impede my vision of the dawning of a new day. The universe will provide me a comfortable sanctuary. I do not rush to the shore to get my feet wet, walking in old footsteps, but I wait for the tide to come to me in its own time savoring the passage.

I will not heed to judgement my ears will listen patiently but not participate in the black and white advice of a closed mind. I search for my own rhythm no longer carried away by the wind and external forces. I am perched on the window whose glass reveals my own silhouette. My heart open and radiating love and warmth to all parts. The enthusiasm of a new beginning and countless memories already so heartfelt. My gratitude is my companion each day as I experience life the way I always knew it was supposed to be.

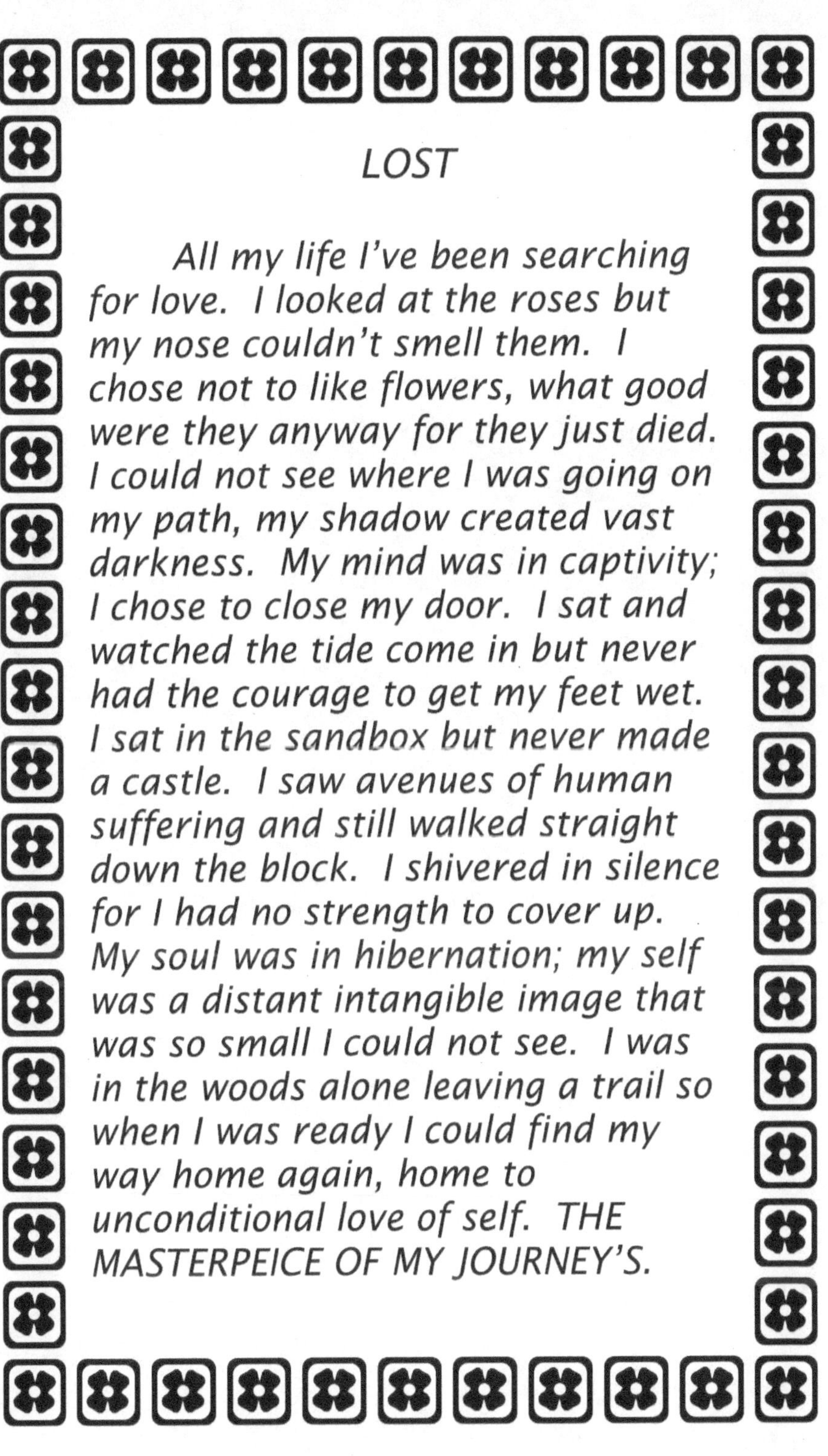

LOST

All my life I've been searching for love. I looked at the roses but my nose couldn't smell them. I chose not to like flowers, what good were they anyway for they just died. I could not see where I was going on my path, my shadow created vast darkness. My mind was in captivity; I chose to close my door. I sat and watched the tide come in but never had the courage to get my feet wet. I sat in the sandbox but never made a castle. I saw avenues of human suffering and still walked straight down the block. I shivered in silence for I had no strength to cover up. My soul was in hibernation; my self was a distant intangible image that was so small I could not see. I was in the woods alone leaving a trail so when I was ready I could find my way home again, home to unconditional love of self. THE MASTERPEICE OF MY JOURNEY'S.

INNER VOICES

Parts of my soul have spoken to me. I'm beginning to understand my harmony. I'm beginning to understand what's inside I no longer want to run and hide. I'm beginning to like what I see inside. It is a whole new world that is opening up for me. I'm beginning to explore my mind and leaving all my insignificant worries behind. I am moving forward; I am living and staying in the moment. I am living for happiness and forgetting sorrow. I cannot alter or change my past but the days ahead can be meaningful and last. I want each day to bring meaning and growth. If I stay on the right path it will be easy for me. Which path is right for me? The one I chose independently. My life is up to me; no one can help or guide me. I am the pilot of my destiny. My choices and decisions will come from inside and be based on my feelings, instincts and drive.

You see if I chose the path with my heart, doubts and inhibitions will no longer play a part. I will be making decisions from within. I will no longer ponder if I took the right advice for the spirit inside of me is my only vice.

ENDLESS JOY

You awaken with love in your heart. Laughter opens the lid of you self-containment. You feel engulfed in the flames of your energy and you don't want to escape. You desire the warmth. Passion free's you from your limitations. Your reflection is one of radiance. Your wisdom and power lights the way for you. You redesign your life in a bright new sky. Endless glory and beauty rain down upon you.

Ominous sky's are behind you. The black of night is a mask you no longer wear. The leaves of your ego have fallen to death. You smile at strangers you extend your arms past the horizons reaching for more. Your capabilities unlimited. Your vision vastly tainted by the prism of a rainbow that only you can see.

A seed fertilized by underground networks and webs of emotional tides. An entity spoken for by spiritual guidance. A door that must remain open to obtain privacy from the world. The internal stirring of thoughts now being judged from new prospective.

The peak of emotional bondage unleashed against the enemies.

Your spirit is felt and is attracted toward the light. I sense a new fragrance that I chose to wear each day with awareness of its potency.

METAMORPHOSIS

Hiding for many years appearing from the darkness to be found. I tiptoe through the grass with caution and fear of being seen or heard. My intuition guides me out, I feel safe with myself for I have become the light; I can shine on my own. What a revelation to see; now my purpose can be revealed to me. The air is warm against my body; I frolic in my space. The aura of clarity hits me I smell the potency of nature. I walk with untraceable steps my patterns defaced. My eyes are closed but I can see that the power I ever needed was buried inside of me.

SACRED JOURNEY

I step out of the shadow into the light, inhibitions no longer held tight. I spend a night inside myself, I spend the night alone. Being released from awareness free to roam. Revealing all the emotions the black and white. Realizing which thoughts are real and which ones are transparent. Recognizing fear and destructive patterns. Trusting and releasing my highest good. Receiving balance and clarity. Embracing the gratefulness of universal love. I am left only with my presence. I am introduced to a part of myself I've never known. A placed filled with love. A place that now emanates my home. A part that was always there uncovered only by the stillness and solitude of my mind.

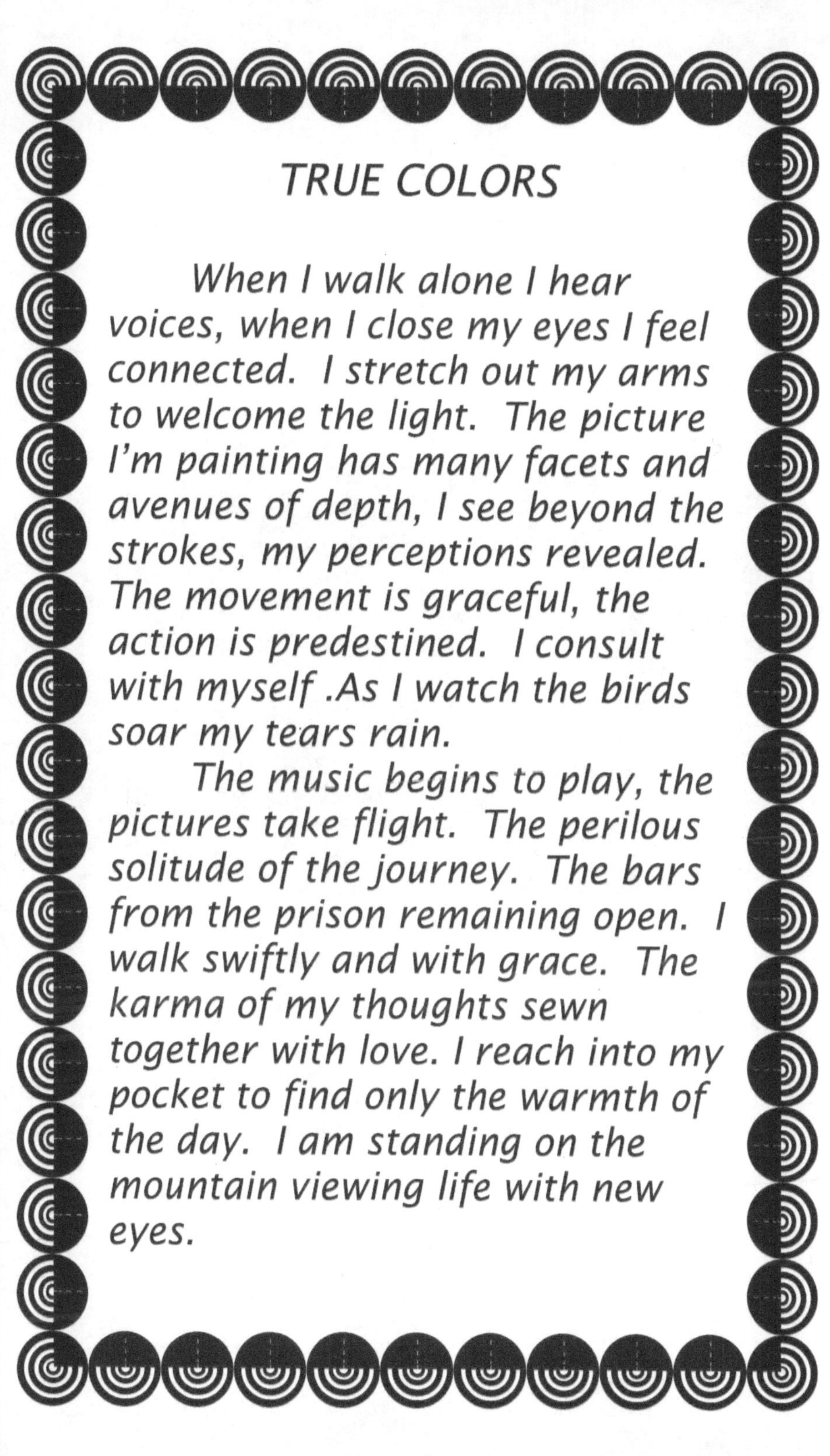

TRUE COLORS

When I walk alone I hear voices, when I close my eyes I feel connected. I stretch out my arms to welcome the light. The picture I'm painting has many facets and avenues of depth, I see beyond the strokes, my perceptions revealed. The movement is graceful, the action is predestined. I consult with myself .As I watch the birds soar my tears rain.

The music begins to play, the pictures take flight. The perilous solitude of the journey. The bars from the prison remaining open. I walk swiftly and with grace. The karma of my thoughts sewn together with love. I reach into my pocket to find only the warmth of the day. I am standing on the mountain viewing life with new eyes.

WHO AM I

I pose the question WHO AM I? I feel it's not black or white, I feel its texture is woven into many different patterns. I feel the intimacy of internal guidance and struggle; I feel my emotions signaling me. My mind encompasses the sorrow with gratitude, but my attitude becomes the centerpiece to which the foliage becomes green or breaks off on its own. My meditations are clearly white. Does my faith bring me down to the stream to see the water visible? Do I float or sink vastly and resurface. Does my body recognize the pattern or am I once again blinded by my shadow. When I speak am I representing me or who I am supposed to be. I lie on the ground stripped of my negativity, my face in the grass relying on my higher power to fertilize me.

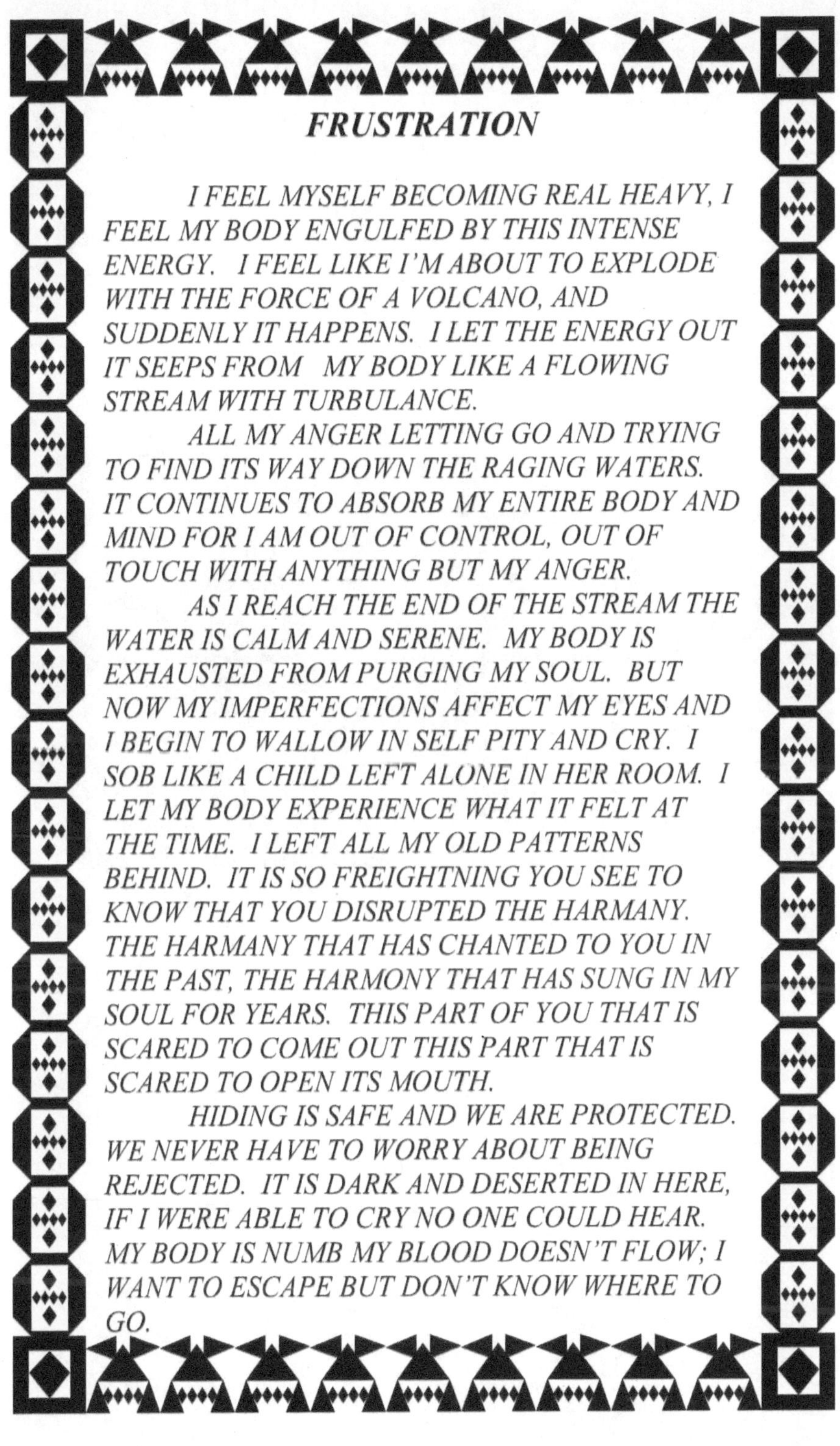

FRUSTRATION

I FEEL MYSELF BECOMING REAL HEAVY, I FEEL MY BODY ENGULFED BY THIS INTENSE ENERGY. I FEEL LIKE I'M ABOUT TO EXPLODE WITH THE FORCE OF A VOLCANO, AND SUDDENLY IT HAPPENS. I LET THE ENERGY OUT IT SEEPS FROM MY BODY LIKE A FLOWING STREAM WITH TURBULANCE.

ALL MY ANGER LETTING GO AND TRYING TO FIND ITS WAY DOWN THE RAGING WATERS. IT CONTINUES TO ABSORB MY ENTIRE BODY AND MIND FOR I AM OUT OF CONTROL, OUT OF TOUCH WITH ANYTHING BUT MY ANGER.

AS I REACH THE END OF THE STREAM THE WATER IS CALM AND SERENE. MY BODY IS EXHAUSTED FROM PURGING MY SOUL. BUT NOW MY IMPERFECTIONS AFFECT MY EYES AND I BEGIN TO WALLOW IN SELF PITY AND CRY. I SOB LIKE A CHILD LEFT ALONE IN HER ROOM. I LET MY BODY EXPERIENCE WHAT IT FELT AT THE TIME. I LEFT ALL MY OLD PATTERNS BEHIND. IT IS SO FREIGHTNING YOU SEE TO KNOW THAT YOU DISRUPTED THE HARMANY. THE HARMANY THAT HAS CHANTED TO YOU IN THE PAST, THE HARMONY THAT HAS SUNG IN MY SOUL FOR YEARS. THIS PART OF YOU THAT IS SCARED TO COME OUT THIS PART THAT IS SCARED TO OPEN ITS MOUTH.

HIDING IS SAFE AND WE ARE PROTECTED. WE NEVER HAVE TO WORRY ABOUT BEING REJECTED. IT IS DARK AND DESERTED IN HERE, IF I WERE ABLE TO CRY NO ONE COULD HEAR. MY BODY IS NUMB MY BLOOD DOESN'T FLOW; I WANT TO ESCAPE BUT DON'T KNOW WHERE TO GO.

REPETITION

I have been doing so well for so long. Why are my old patterns still hanging on? Why are they waiting to reappear? Why do they always seem so near? Why do the minute I weaken they invade my mind and body?

I need to be strong and regain composure. I need to not let my old patterns get any exposure. I feel they are always there hiding waiting to come out. My mind gets fogged I become confused and suddenly I have no options which to chose. My mind is blank my awareness is gone; I become depressed and can't move on. I want to cry for help and to be saved, I want someone to come get me and take me away. Away to where it is safe, away to where it is calm, away to where again I can move on. Starting again is so hard to do your old patterns have made everything foreign to you. Why aren't your new patterns waiting to reappear? Why is it so hard to think clear? Why do we have to feel as though we are starting over again instead of continuing on? Why do we feel like all the progress we made in the past is gone?

So like a ship at sea we begin to wander around aimlessly in search of our dreams and goals. They are the compass that will lead us in the right way, they are the spirit inside of us each day. So I will set sail again and map my course and I will never look back with any remorse.

GROWTH

Some days I sit inside myself alone, feeling like I am trapped feeling like it is forsaken for me to leave. Ideation's of abstract images of familiarity breed within me. The outside world so near but yet so far. I see the forced entry in which I passed. I feel unpleasant waves of emotional tides washing through me. I am treading in the rough waters appraised of the approaching storm. Tears fill my eyes for I have swum the current before. My strength again tested for that which I have not learned. The realization of my frequent visits are reminders of the humility my ego must capture. I refuse to sink to the rocky bottom, for I have been cut and injured by indulgences of self-pity and guilt before. I may not be visible but I am viable and I will resurface again.

PASSAGES OF TIME

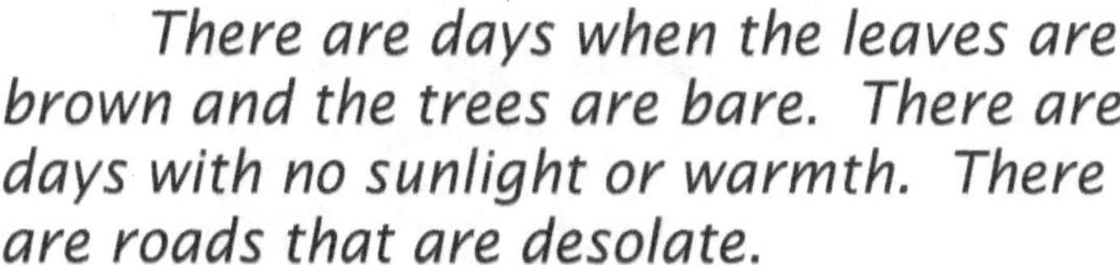

There are days when the leaves are brown and the trees are bare. There are days with no sunlight or warmth. There are roads that are desolate.

There is stillness breathing effortlessly.

The leaves fallen to death awaiting the breeze to change patterns and recreate movement.

There are days when the sky is endless with beauty, when the air is crisp and vibrant.

When you feel the energy and surrender to the current.
When love becomes your protective layer.
When laughter turns to tears of gratitude.
When messages echo with reverence.
When the bridge collapses after you cross.
When you swing through the fire feeling no warmth.
When you jump on your own without signaling.
When you land on your feet in an unknown territory

A new journey has begun.

Reflection of a Stranger

When I look in the mirror what do I see? What I see is a stranger that's me. Who is this girl, who is this woman? I know it is me but who am I? How come I can't look myself in the eye, How come I get chills and start to cry. How can I be a stranger to my own soul? How can I have trouble saying my own name. Am I scared to look for what I might see, is my unconscious trying to hide me. I feel there is a protective wall around me which keeps me from giving away all my energy. I feel as though I can't express myself genuinely, I feel like there is an obstacle course in front of me and If I take the right paths I will get to the real me. But the paths I chose are not always right this is where it becomes hard not to give up the fight, this is where it is hard to get back on track. You see this is what my self-awareness lacks. It lacks insight and direction, it lacks forgiveness and awareness, it lacks courage and feeds on despair. If I continue this way I will go no where. I have to awaken my spirit to explore my body and to become fully attuned with the meditations of my heart. I feel that this is atleast where I can start.

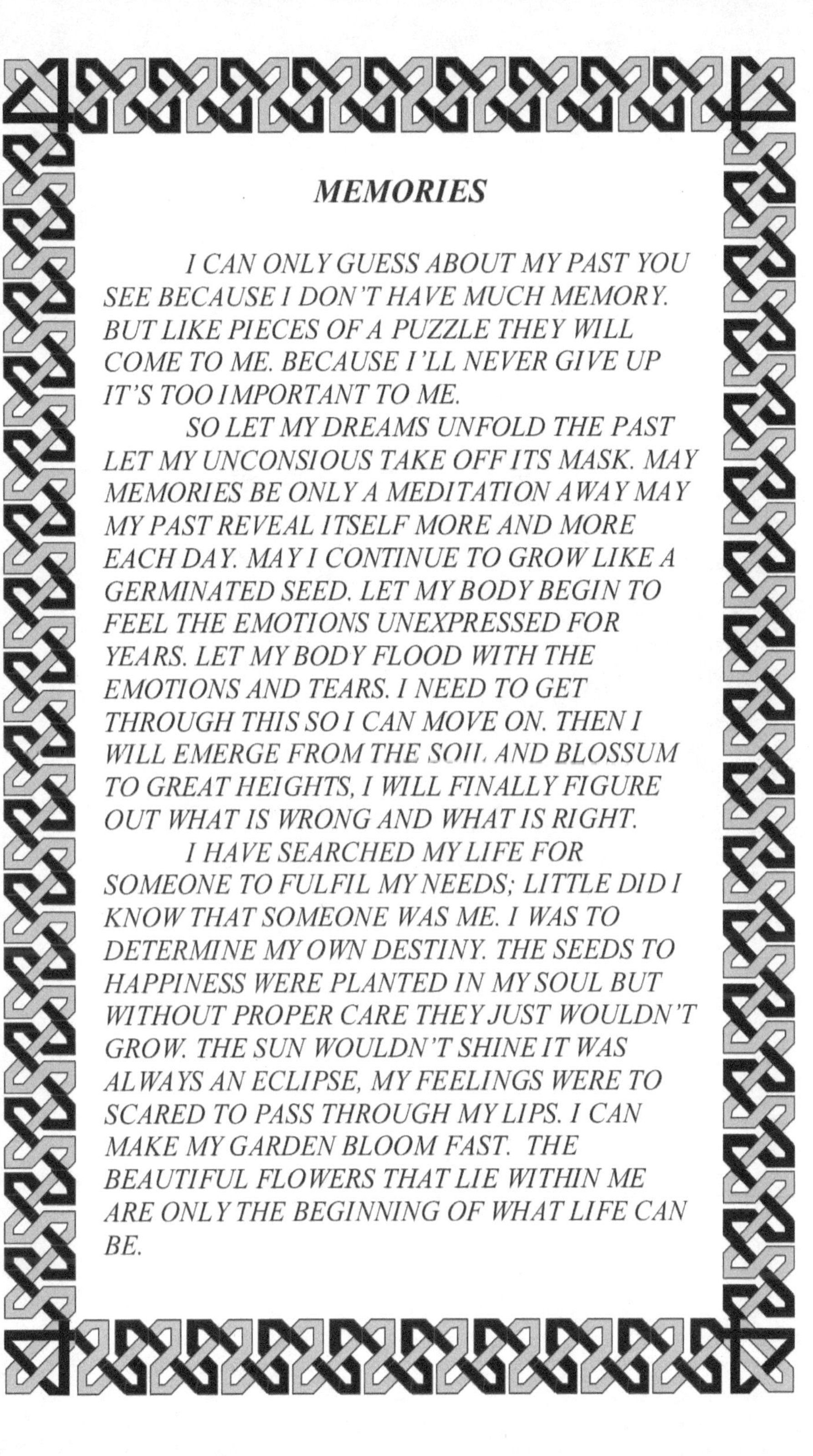

MEMORIES

I CAN ONLY GUESS ABOUT MY PAST YOU SEE BECAUSE I DON'T HAVE MUCH MEMORY. BUT LIKE PIECES OF A PUZZLE THEY WILL COME TO ME. BECAUSE I'LL NEVER GIVE UP IT'S TOO IMPORTANT TO ME.

SO LET MY DREAMS UNFOLD THE PAST LET MY UNCONSIOUS TAKE OFF ITS MASK. MAY MEMORIES BE ONLY A MEDITATION AWAY MAY MY PAST REVEAL ITSELF MORE AND MORE EACH DAY. MAY I CONTINUE TO GROW LIKE A GERMINATED SEED. LET MY BODY BEGIN TO FEEL THE EMOTIONS UNEXPRESSED FOR YEARS. LET MY BODY FLOOD WITH THE EMOTIONS AND TEARS. I NEED TO GET THROUGH THIS SO I CAN MOVE ON. THEN I WILL EMERGE FROM THE SOIL AND BLOSSUM TO GREAT HEIGHTS, I WILL FINALLY FIGURE OUT WHAT IS WRONG AND WHAT IS RIGHT.

I HAVE SEARCHED MY LIFE FOR SOMEONE TO FULFIL MY NEEDS; LITTLE DID I KNOW THAT SOMEONE WAS ME. I WAS TO DETERMINE MY OWN DESTINY. THE SEEDS TO HAPPINESS WERE PLANTED IN MY SOUL BUT WITHOUT PROPER CARE THEY JUST WOULDN'T GROW. THE SUN WOULDN'T SHINE IT WAS ALWAYS AN ECLIPSE, MY FEELINGS WERE TO SCARED TO PASS THROUGH MY LIPS. I CAN MAKE MY GARDEN BLOOM FAST. THE BEAUTIFUL FLOWERS THAT LIE WITHIN ME ARE ONLY THE BEGINNING OF WHAT LIFE CAN BE.

IN THE SPIRIT OF THE MOMENT

Regression sneaks up on us and blinds us like the sun when we become weak. It's almost like a spirit waiting to feel the negative energy that invites itself in each and every time. But the question is do we fear or welcome the spirit.

If we fear it we must always be on guard and arrange our lives in sequence. It requires significant energy and exhausts us. Is it normal to be so physically exhausted at the end of the day and feel that our lives are just fading away? Are we so out of touch with whom we are that our thoughts hover on only tomorrow? What happened to today, did it just pass and fade away. Did we feel anything, did we learn or grow or were we just constantly on the go. Did you notice the sky, did you notice the breeze, did you notice the beautiful flowers that were right next to the trees. Did you hear the birds sing? Did you watch the children play, did you wish that you could have enjoyed today. Living in the present isn't really hard to do, if you open your eyes and just take a look around you, being aware is being in control, it's letting your mind expand, nurture and continue to grow. If we go through life with our eyes closed when we come to an obstacle we can only guess which way to go. I choose to be alert, I choose to be aware. Being in the moment is much more precious than gold. Any gift that you get from within will only prosper and grow.

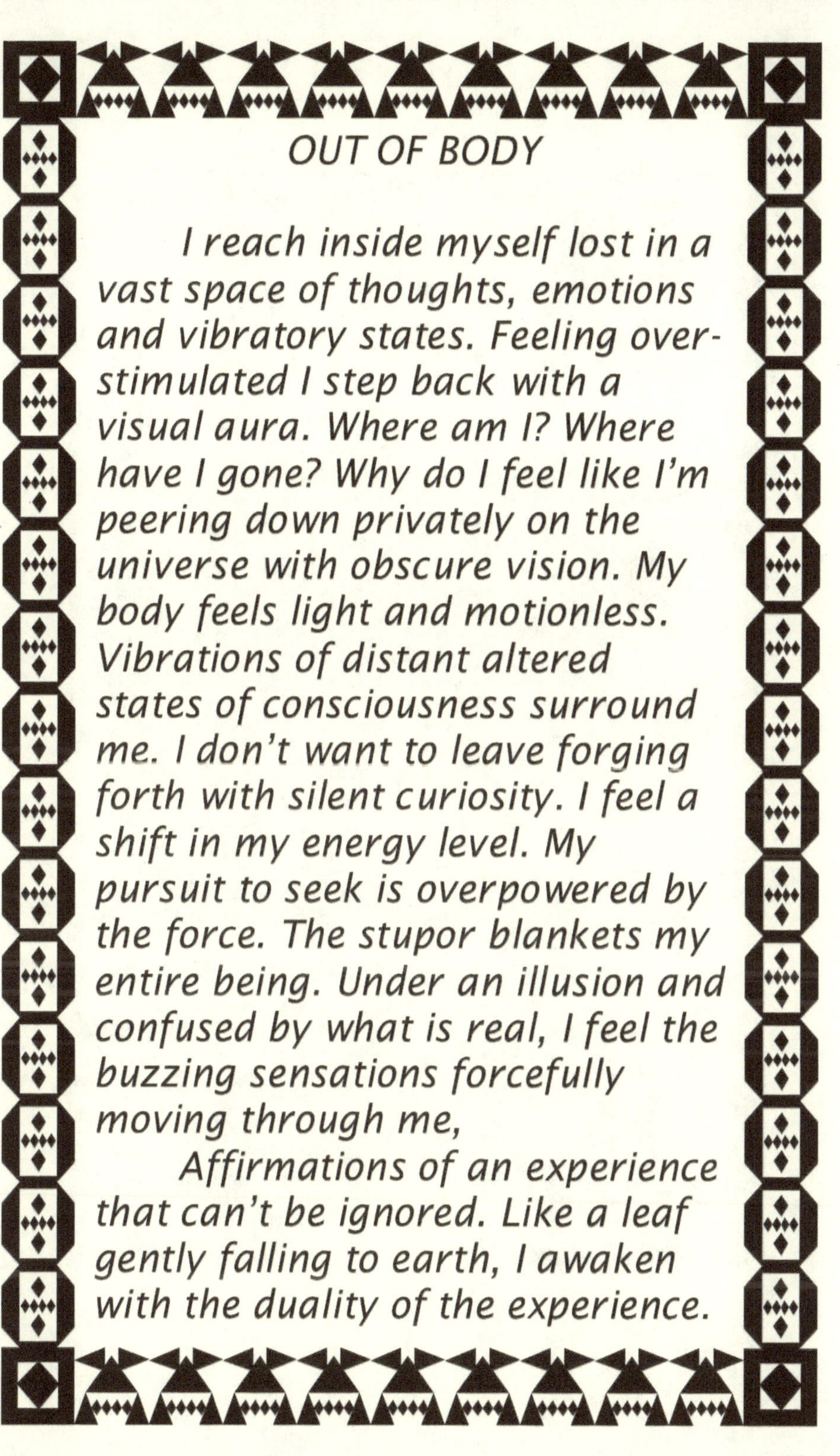

OUT OF BODY

I reach inside myself lost in a vast space of thoughts, emotions and vibratory states. Feeling over-stimulated I step back with a visual aura. Where am I? Where have I gone? Why do I feel like I'm peering down privately on the universe with obscure vision. My body feels light and motionless. Vibrations of distant altered states of consciousness surround me. I don't want to leave forging forth with silent curiosity. I feel a shift in my energy level. My pursuit to seek is overpowered by the force. The stupor blankets my entire being. Under an illusion and confused by what is real, I feel the buzzing sensations forcefully moving through me,

Affirmations of an experience that can't be ignored. Like a leaf gently falling to earth, I awaken with the duality of the experience.

THE DARK VOID

I sit to contemplate this moment of life, an unwanted feeling one of distant nature seems to hold me tight. I am embraced by a false sense of security. I feel its intent surrounding me and obstructing my view. I feel it trying to quench my thirst for knowledge. It stays with me as my companion guiding me through its darkness. I feel obscure, as I am lead across unwillingly. I try to rest but it manifests constant images in my dreams. I awaken my body heavy and slow as if I had been running through time. My mind searching for acceptance of its purpose. My mind waiting for the gift of light.

THOUGHTS OF THE DAY

I find myself lost in my own mind. The stimulus of overwhelming voices all wanting to be heard. I filter my hearing running toward the positive with the breath of its opposite tracing my steps. I stop to pause and rest and begin again. My inner strength camouflaged by the desires of voices I don't recognize. I feel torn into a kaleidoscope of demands for my attention, my senses challenged changing my energy with each call. I feel lightheaded while being carried away by the winds of the ominous sky. Without direction I wonder aimlessly through the dense fog before me. Each voice tugging at my rope with masked intentions. The clarity arises when the sun's rays are seen. Through the shadow I feel stillness and the vastness of the area that lies before me, the journey that will determine the fragility of my will.

Clarity can only be seen with your eyes closed.

THE JOURNEY INSIDE BEGINS "SKEPTICISM"

Skepticism immerses you but you ask your ego to let go, your mind to stay open, your heart to feel. You close you eyes to ask you higher self to embrace the moment with passion. You listen with deaf ears you search for silence. The warmth begins to cover you and protection becomes awareness, existing by the flows and currents and channeling of the breath. Joy is felt and a new territory has been claimed. After effects hit you with spontaneity leaving you lightheaded with a crown of jewels only to be treasured by you. You realize the gift and how it has changed your life. You accept it with grace and deep appreciation. A precious gift toward self.

FAITH

*What keeps you going when all
else fails?
The hopes and dreams that have
not yet been fulfilled. The love
that you are so eager to share, the
soul, which is ready to open.*

*Like a caterpillar waiting to
spread it wings.
Like a melody a cappella.
How does the light shine through
the darkness at the end of the
day?
How do you prepare to guide
yourself through another day?*

*Your path is simply opening its
doors for you.
Take faith by the hand and walk
right through.*

The Gift of Life

You awaken each day with a gift from the divine. A blessing from above you adore and cherish, you see the beauty of yourself recreated. You look into her eyes and you sense love. She longs for your guidance and advice. She mirrors your faults as well as your beauty. Your task as a mother the most important in your life. You look at her in wonder at the beautiful child before you. Her eyes glow like stars in the night, her smile brightens up my day. I feel so proud when I hold her hand. I feel a love beyond words. I thank god each day for the most precious gift I could receive. I pray for patience, strength and love to surround me each day, so that I can fill her heart and soul with the gift of my endless unconditional love.

DOUGLAS

I dreamed of you many times in my head. The adoration of your very presence renews me and opens up a window that the view is breathtaking. I feel a stirring of emotion that shines through my ivory skin. I sense an awareness of self, I sense beauty, I sense love.

Renewed vines of hope and strength branch out to show my growth and expansion. I look in the mirror and see a different face, my reflection no longer transparent. As I move through the world I become more than a spectator. I refuse to listen with deaf ears, I refuse to close my mind or heart again. The unlimited use of energy and karma redirecting me. The songs of my heart gracefully singing with the voice of true spirit.

I feel passion shine rays of light where it was once dark. I can feel your presence with me. I feel you take my hand ever so gently. I feel you caressing me. I love you exactly the way you are. Your tenderness navigates through my soul. I have been given a gift that will forever rain down on me. My endless love of you will forever resonate through my body each day here forth.

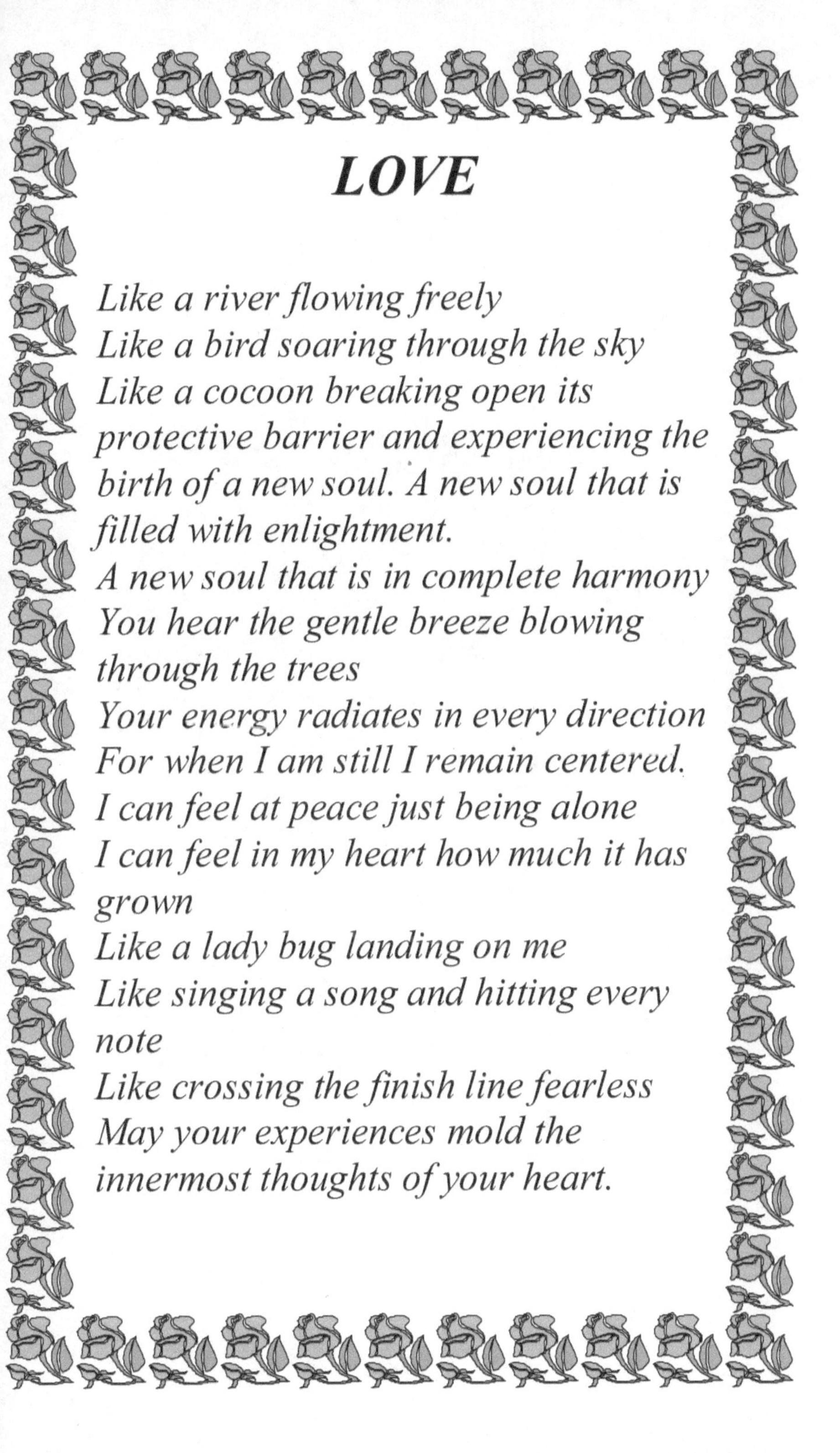

LOVE

Like a river flowing freely
Like a bird soaring through the sky
Like a cocoon breaking open its
protective barrier and experiencing the
birth of a new soul. A new soul that is
filled with enlightment.
A new soul that is in complete harmony
You hear the gentle breeze blowing
through the trees
Your energy radiates in every direction
For when I am still I remain centered.
I can feel at peace just being alone
I can feel in my heart how much it has
grown
Like a lady bug landing on me
Like singing a song and hitting every
note
Like crossing the finish line fearless
May your experiences mold the
innermost thoughts of your heart.

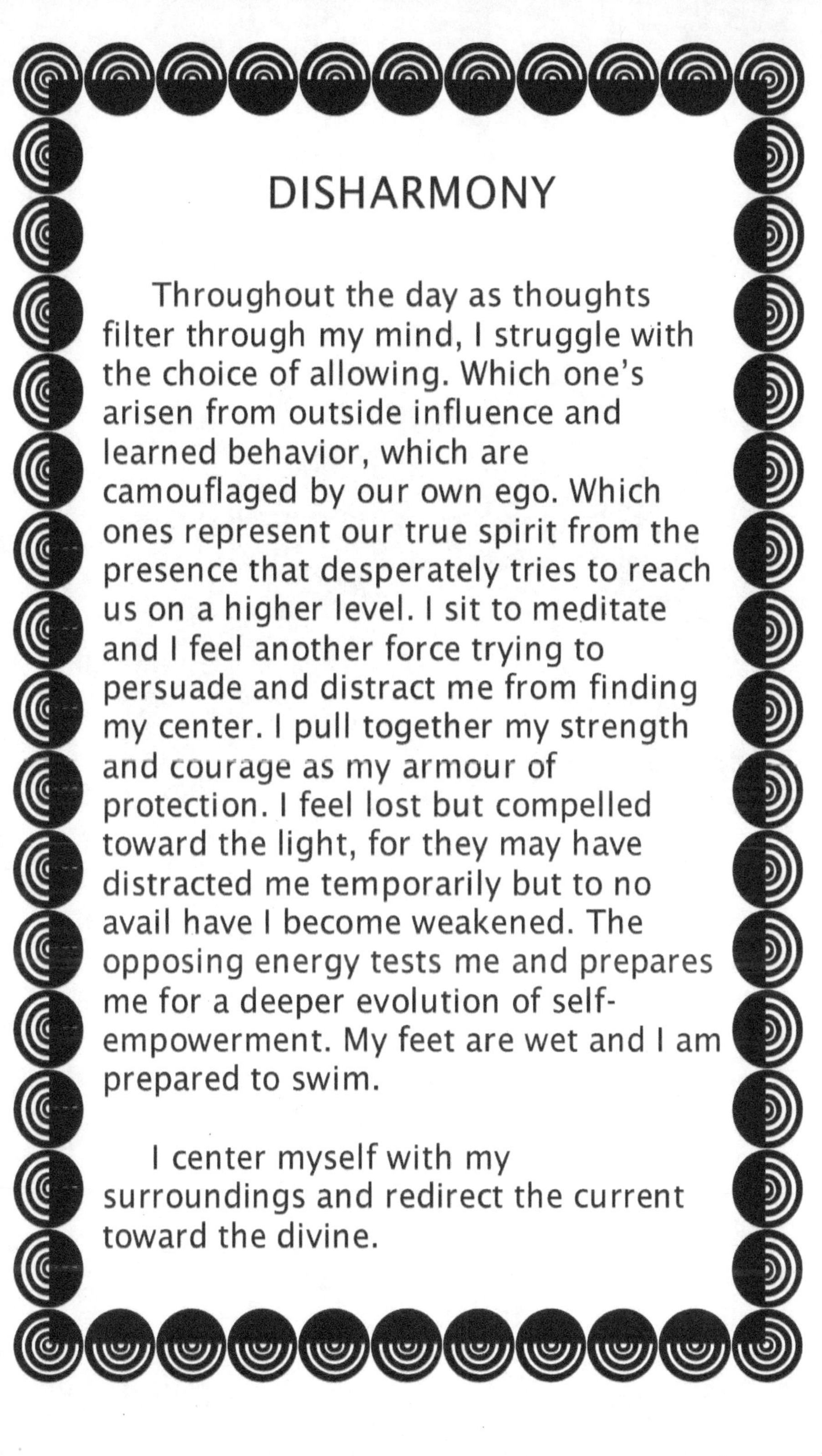

DISHARMONY

Throughout the day as thoughts filter through my mind, I struggle with the choice of allowing. Which one's arisen from outside influence and learned behavior, which are camouflaged by our own ego. Which ones represent our true spirit from the presence that desperately tries to reach us on a higher level. I sit to meditate and I feel another force trying to persuade and distract me from finding my center. I pull together my strength and courage as my armour of protection. I feel lost but compelled toward the light, for they may have distracted me temporarily but to no avail have I become weakened. The opposing energy tests me and prepares me for a deeper evolution of self-empowerment. My feet are wet and I am prepared to swim.

I center myself with my surroundings and redirect the current toward the divine.

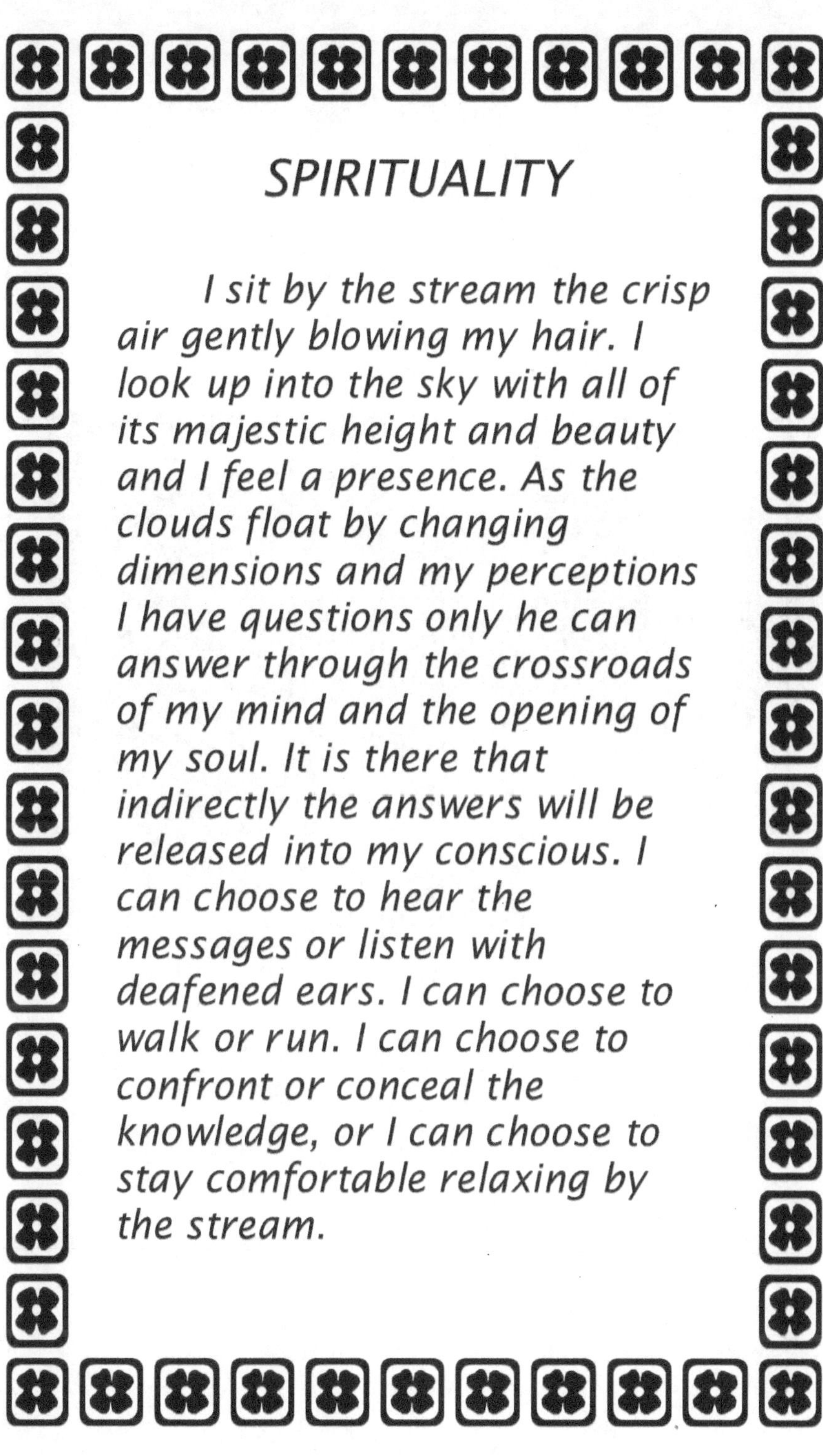

SPIRITUALITY

I sit by the stream the crisp air gently blowing my hair. I look up into the sky with all of its majestic height and beauty and I feel a presence. As the clouds float by changing dimensions and my perceptions I have questions only he can answer through the crossroads of my mind and the opening of my soul. It is there that indirectly the answers will be released into my conscious. I can choose to hear the messages or listen with deafened ears. I can choose to walk or run. I can choose to confront or conceal the knowledge, or I can choose to stay comfortable relaxing by the stream.

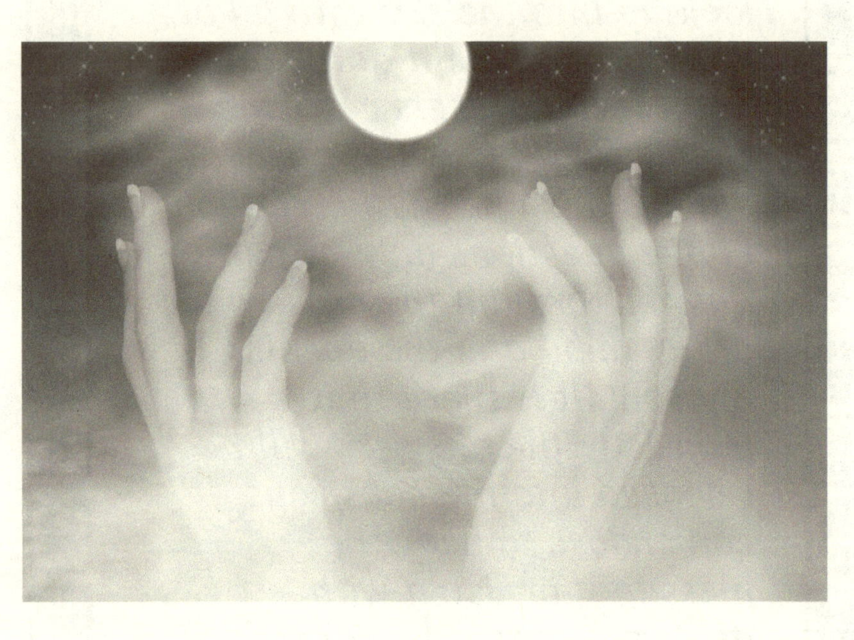

NOURISHMENT

Memories of love we share. Memories of pain and despair. Memories of future expectations and dreams are surfacing.

Today I will move forth with vigor any negativity stripped from me. I am strong I am ready.

There are no wrong decisions I will learn and grow from every experience good or bad. I will attune myself to that of the universe. I will prevail with my own thoughts untainted by others judgments and criticisms. I will follow my heart. I will follow my soul.

www.ingramcontent.com/pod-product-compliance
Lightning Source LLC
LaVergne TN
LVHW050946080826
845145LV00004B/1429

* 9 7 8 1 9 3 4 1 9 4 2 0 1 *